D1649195

Bar Code®:
Serving Alcohol Responsibly

SERVER GUIDE

Serving beverage alcohol responsibly means helping your guests enjoy beverage alcohol's pleasant aspects while safeguarding them from the unpleasant, and possibly dangerous, effects of drinking too much.

National Restaurant Association
THE EDUCATIONAL FOUNDATION

Disclaimer

The information presented in this resource book has been compiled from sources and documents believed to be reliable and represents the best professional judgment of The Educational Foundation of the National Restaurant Association. However, the accuracy of the information presented is not guaranteed, nor is any responsibility assumed or implied by The Educational Foundation for any damage or loss resulting from inaccuracies or omissions.

Laws may vary greatly by city, county, and state. This book is not intended to provide legal advice or establish standards of reasonable behavior. Operators who develop beverage alcohol-related policies and procedures as part of their commitment to employee and customer safety are urged to use the advice and guidance of legal counsel.

Marianne Gajewski, Director of Product Development

Susan M. Myers, Manager, Risk Management, Product Development

Virginia A. Christopher, Manager, Production

Michael E. Johnson, Group Product Manager

Ellen M. Ross, Associate Editor, Risk Management, Product Development

Beverly E. Sorkin, Associate Editor, Risk Management, Product Development

Laura Stone, Creative Manager

Thomas Armstrong, Ph.D, Writer, Candace Frawley & Associates

Cover Design, Mark Oldach Design, Ltd.

Cover Photography, Arcerio Photography, Inc.

Bar Code®: Serving Alcohol Responsibly
Server Guide

Copyright © 1996 by The Educational Foundation of the National Restaurant Association.

ISBN: 1-883904-51-X

Inventory Code: E412

All rights reserved. No part of this document may be reproduced, stored in a retrieval system, or transmitted in any form or by any means, electronic, mechanical, photocopying, recording, or otherwise, without the prior written consent of the publisher.

Printed in the U.S.A.

10 9 8

On behalf of the people in the foodservice industry who will benefit, The Educational Foundation of the National Restaurant Association is pleased to thank our *Bar Code®: Serving Alcohol Responsibly* sponsor for the financial support which has made possible the development of this book.

Anheuser-Busch Companies, Inc.

Acknowledgments

The development of the *Bar Code®: Serving Alcohol Responsibly Server Guide* would not have been possible without the expertise of our many advisors and manuscript reviewers. The Educational Foundation of the National Restaurant Association is pleased to thank the following people for the time and effort they dedicated to this project:

Moshen Azizsoltani; University of Nevada, Las Vegas

Steve Baker; Applebee's International, Inc.

Stephen Barth, J.D.; University of Houston

Peter C. Crafts; Massachusetts Restaurant Association

H.A. Divine, Ph.D, CHA, FMP; University of Denver

Wayne Gatewood; Donatos Pizza

Thomas W. Gathers; Uno Restaurant Corporation

John Kaestner; Anheuser-Busch Companies, Inc.

John Marcello, R.S.; The Educational Foundation
of the National Restaurant Association

Steve Prentice; Illinois Restaurant Association

Deborah Ruemler; Red Lobster Restaurants

John E.H. Sherry; Cornell University

TABLE OF CONTENTS

INTRODUCTION

The purpose of the *Bar Code®: Serving Alcohol Responsibly* program is to help you and your co-workers responsibly serve beverage alcohol as part of the total service experience you provide for your guests.

What Is Serving Beverage Alcohol Responsibly?

For many people, beverage alcohol has been a pleasurable addition to life. **Serving beverage alcohol responsibly** means helping your guests enjoy beverage alcohol's pleasant aspects while safeguarding them from the unpleasant, and possibly dangerous, effects of drinking too much.

A server's key tasks are to monitor guests, appropriately serve them beverage alcohol, and safely deal with any undesirable beverage alcohol-related incidents. A server also is responsible for the following tasks:

♦ Obeying laws prohibiting serving beverage alcohol to minors and intoxicated individuals.

♦ Following standardized beverage alcohol service policies to avoid serving a guest too much beverage alcohol.

♦ Keeping track of how much a guest drinks and observing any behavioral changes.

♦ Slowing or stopping beverage alcohol service to guests when necessary.

♦ **Not** allowing an intoxicated guest to drive away from an establishment.

Why Is Responsible Beverage Alcohol Service Important?

Beverage alcohol is an important source of income for hospitality establishments and their employees. Unfortunately, overconsuming beverage alcohol can cause problems for everyone. Responsible beverage alcohol service is simply good service— serving guests what they want in the safest, most enjoyable way possible. Serving beverage alcohol responsibly is important because:

♦ People who have consumed too much beverage alcohol can become unpleasant, uncoordinated, or can get sick. An intoxicated individual can become abusive, start fights, and injure other guests. If guests do not feel safe in your establishment, they will not visit your establishment.

♦ Cities and states are increasing drunk driving penalties.

♦ In most states, an establishment and its employees can be held liable for a guest's behavior after the guest consumes beverage alcohol.

The Benefits of Serving Beverage Alcohol Responsibly

Responsible beverage alcohol service safeguards your guests, your community, yourself, your co-workers, and your establishment by reducing drunk driving crashes and other injuries related to beverage alcohol overconsumption. When guests responsibly consume beverage alcohol, they tend to stay longer, order more food and beverages, and leave larger tips. Overall, responsible beverage alcohol service makes your establishment a better place to work and visit.

Careful planning, good training, and teamwork are the keys to safe and responsible beverage alcohol service. By staying informed about responsible beverage alcohol service policies, you can provide your guests with excellent service and then reap the benefits.

Getting the Most from *Bar Code*

The *Server Guide* covers basic information for you to preview before attending your training session. The terms alcohol and beverage alcohol are used throughout the *Server Guide*.

In the *Server Guide*, **alcohol** is the ingredient in beverage alcohol that can cause intoxication and **beverage alcohol** is what a person consumes.

Words you need to know are bolded and defined in the *Glossary* in the back of the *Server Guide*. There are exercises at the end of *Chapters 1, 2, 3, and 4* and an *Answer Key* in the back of the *Server Guide*. So you will better understand the material, complete these exercises before going to the training session.

In the training session, you will discuss the course material with your co-workers. Learning together is a positive first step toward using your responsible beverage alcohol service skills.

Note: Icons appear throughout the *Server Guide* to emphasize important beverage alcohol service information. The icons are:

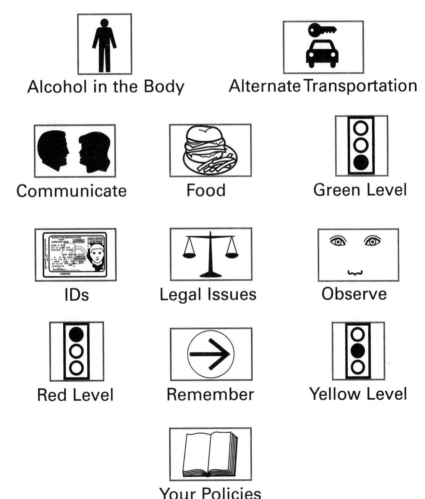

Alcohol in the Body	Alternate Transportation

Communicate	Food	Green Level

IDs	Legal Issues	Observe

Red Level	Remember	Yellow Level

Your Policies

HOW ALCOHOL AFFECTS THE BODY

Test Your Responsible Beverage Alcohol Service IQ

1. **True or False:** One 12-ounce beer contains less alcohol than a 1¼-ounce shot of 80-proof whiskey. (See *Composition of Drinks*, page 5.)

2. **True or False:** The liver can process about one drink an hour. (See *Alcohol's Path through the Body*, page 6.)

3. **True or False:** Coffee helps the liver metabolize alcohol. (See *Alcohol's Path through the Body*, page 6.)

4. **True or False:** Alcohol is a stimulant that energizes the body's vital functions. (See *Alcohol's Effects on the Body*, page 9.)

5. **True or False:** In general, women become intoxicated more slowly and can tolerate more alcohol than men. (See *Factors Affecting Alcohol Absorption*, page 10.)

Learning Objectives

After completing this chapter, you should be able to:

◆ Calculate drink equivalencies and figure out how much alcohol a guest has consumed.

◆ Trace alcohol's path through the body and understand how alcohol affects the body.

◆ List the factors that control the body's absorption of alcohol.

◆ Recognize certain behaviors to estimate how much beverage alcohol a guest has consumed and how much more he or she can safely consume.

Introduction

The way people react to alcohol depends on how much they consume, how much enters the bloodstream, and how fast it enters the bloodstream. To protect your guests, you need to know what affects the body's absorption of alcohol, the behaviors associated with beverage alcohol consumption, and how much beverage alcohol a person can safely consume.

How Beverage Alcohol Is Made and Rated

Beverage alcohol is made by fermenting plants, such as berries, fruits, or grains. During **fermentation**, tiny life-forms called **micro-organisms**, such as yeasts, break down the plant's molecules and produce alcohol. Beer and wine are examples of beverage alcohol that **only** undergo a fermentation process. **Distilled spirits or liquors**, such as scotch, bourbon, gin, vodka, and rum, also undergo distillation. During **distillation**, water is removed from the alcohol to make it stronger.

Beverage alcohol is rated by proof and percentage of alcohol. The percentage of alcohol can be determined by dividing the proof in half. For example:

80-proof liquor ÷ 2 = 40 percent alcohol.

100-proof liquor ÷ 2 = 50 percent alcohol.

An important part of responsible beverage alcohol service is knowing how much alcohol is in the drinks you serve.

Composition of Drinks

Each of the following drinks contains about ½ ounce of pure alcohol despite differences in their size and content.

♦ A 12-ounce glass of beer. (In general, ice beers have a higher percentage of alcohol.)

♦ A 4-ounce glass of wine.

♦ A straight (containing only beverage alcohol) drink or a mixed drink made with 1¼ ounces of 80-proof liquor.

◆ A straight drink or a mixed drink made with 1 ounce of 100-proof liquor.

12 oz. beer = 4 oz. wine
= 1¼ oz. 80-proof liquor
= 1 oz. 100-proof liquor

Use these comparisons to estimate how much alcohol a guest has consumed. Always be alert for several other factors that can affect the strength of a drink.

◆ Liqueurs and cordials. Some **liqueurs** and **cordials** contain 20 percent alcohol, while others can contain almost as much alcohol as whiskeys (40 percent).

◆ Drinks made with a higher-proof alcohol, such as 150-proof rum (75 percent alcohol).

◆ Drinks made with double the amount of liquor, such as martinis and Manhattans.

◆ Size of the glass.

◆ Size of the serving poured.

Note: Throughout this *Server Guide*, **drink** refers to any beverage containing the equivalent of ½ ounce of pure alcohol.

Alcohol's Path through the Body

As alcohol moves through the body, its effects depend on how much is consumed, how much of it enters the **bloodstream**, which is the blood circulating through a person's body, and how fast it enters the bloodstream (see *Exhibit 1.1*). Alcohol moves through the body as follows:

1. From the Mouth to the Bloodstream.

   When alcohol is swallowed, small amounts directly enter the bloodstream through **capillaries**, tiny blood vessels, in the mouth. Most of the alcohol flows to the stomach. In the stomach, close to 20 percent of the alcohol can be absorbed directly into the bloodstream. The remaining 80 percent passes to the small intestine where it is absorbed into the bloodstream.

2. Through the Bloodstream to the Entire Body.

Once in the bloodstream, alcohol rapidly spreads through the entire body. Because it dissolves in water and can easily pass through cell walls, alcohol reaches almost all body tissues and cells. Within three minutes of beverage alcohol consumption, the brain accurately determines the amount of alcohol in the bloodstream. A **breathalyzer** accurately measures a person's **blood alcohol content** or **concentration (BAC)** by testing his or her breath. BAC is the percentage of alcohol absorbed into the bloodstream. A BAC of 0.10, the legal level of intoxication in some states, is the equivalent of 1 drop of alcohol in 1,000 drops of blood. If a person's BAC rises to 0.30, he or she can go into a coma. A BAC of 0.40 can result in death.

The legal level of intoxication in my state is a BAC of: _____.

3. Through the Body to the Liver

Once alcohol spreads through the body, most of it must be metabolized (broken down) by the liver. The liver metabolizes alcohol at a constant rate—about one drink per hour. If a person has more than one drink per hour, the liver **cannot** metabolize the alcohol at a quicker rate. The unmetabolized alcohol continues to circulate through the bloodstream and can affect the drinker's mood and behavior.

Note: Drinking coffee, taking a cold shower, or exercising will **not** help the liver metabolize alcohol at a faster rate. At best, an intoxicated person drinking non-alcohol beverages, such as coffee, will stop drinking beverage alcohol, increase the amount of liquid in his or her body, and allow some time to pass before doing other activities, such as driving.

Exhibit 1.1 Alcohol's Path through the Body

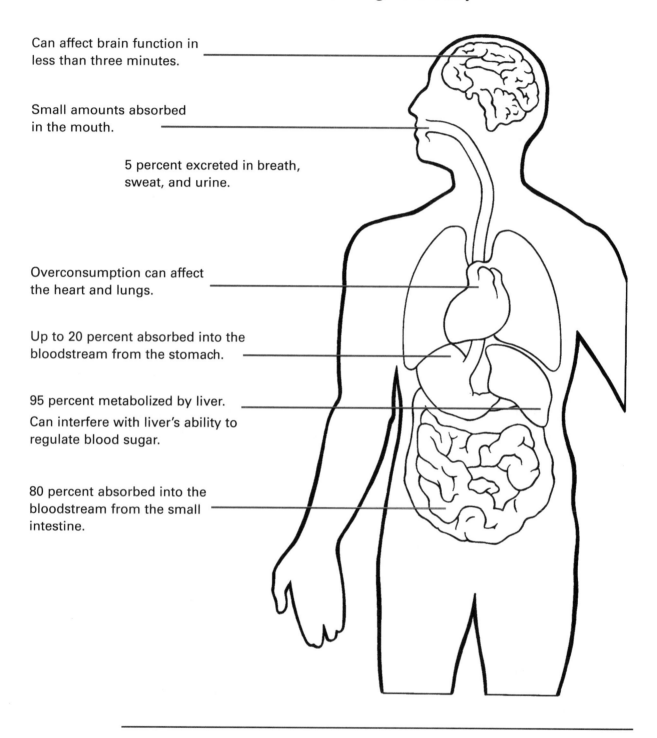

Can affect brain function in less than three minutes.

Small amounts absorbed in the mouth.

5 percent excreted in breath, sweat, and urine.

Overconsumption can affect the heart and lungs.

Up to 20 percent absorbed into the bloodstream from the stomach.

95 percent metabolized by liver. Can interfere with liver's ability to regulate blood sugar.

80 percent absorbed into the bloodstream from the small intestine.

Remember: Time is the key. Allowing the liver enough time to break down alcohol is the **only** way to remove alcohol from the body.

Alcohol's Effects on the Body

The human body is very sensitive to alcohol that is absorbed into the bloodstream. Only a small amount of alcohol is needed for a person to experience a pleasant glow or relaxed inhibitions. An **inhibition** is a mental or psychological process that restrains or suppresses a person's emotions, actions, or thoughts.

Alcohol can act as a:

◆ **Depressant.** A **depressant** is a substance that reduces muscle or nerve activity. Alcohol directly affects the body's central nervous system. Because one of the first areas of the brain affected by alcohol controls a person's inhibitions, beverage alcohol is sometimes incorrectly considered a stimulant. However, as more alcohol is absorbed into the bloodstream, other areas of the brain—judgment, memory, coordination, sensory perception, and major motor skills—become depressed. The depressant effect of alcohol can make driving, or any task in which safety is an issue, a dangerous activity.

◆ **Diuretic.** A **diuretic** is a substance that helps the body lose fluids and causes the sensation of thirst. Alcohol's diuretic effects do not remove a significant amount of alcohol from the body. Because alcohol's diuretic effects can make a guest thirsty, he or she may want to drink more beverage alcohol. Be sure to offer water with all beverage alcohol.

◆ **Vasodilator.** Alcohol causes the small blood vessels on the surface of the skin to dilate (swell). This is called **vasodilation** which results in a loss of body heat. Although the person drinking beverage alcohol feels the vasodilation as heat and flushed skin, his or her body is actually cooling, not warming. Guests who have consumed beverage alcohol should wear adequate clothing during cold weather.

Alcohol can cause:

◆ **Hypoglycemia.** Alcohol disturbs the blood sugar levels in the body causing **hypoglycemia**, a decrease of sugar in the blood. Normally, the liver maintains the body's blood sugar. When alcohol is in the body, the liver must give priority to metabolizing the alcohol. For the average person, a drop in the body's blood sugar due to beverage alcohol consumption can cause hunger, a headache, nausea, and a hangover.

◆ **Digestive changes.** Alcohol initially increases one's appetite, but later decreases it. When beverage alcohol is in the stomach, it can slow or stop food digestion. Before the point of intoxication, food can protect the stomach from alcohol-related irritation. Always offer guests food when serving beverage alcohol.

Factors Affecting Alcohol Absorption

Almost all of the effects of alcohol previously described depend in part on how rapidly alcohol is absorbed into the body. You should know the factors influencing alcohol absorption and use that knowledge when serving guests.

Amount of Alcohol Consumed and Time of Consumption

As a guest consumes more beverage alcohol, the amount absorbed into the bloodstream increases. Remember the following when serving beverage alcohol:

◆ If wine is served in an 8-ounce glass, it will contain approximately twice the amount of alcohol as a 4-ounce glass of wine (one drink) and should be counted as two drinks rather than one. It is a good idea to use smaller wine glasses and limit a glass of wine to four or five ounces.

◆ Since the liver metabolizes about one drink an hour, consuming more than one drink an hour will increase the amount of alcohol absorbed into a guest's bloodstream. Alcohol can build up in the bloodstream and affect a guest long after he or she has stopped drinking.

A guest's BAC can continue to rise even after he or she stops drinking and leaves your establishment. Although the guest appears fine when leaving, he or she can become intoxicated

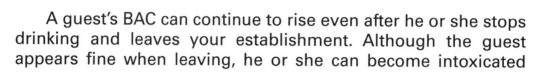

while driving home. For a guest's safety, do not serve doubles or drinks containing two or more liquors, such as Long Island iced teas, martinis, or Manhattans, at last call.

Food

Offering food with beverage alcohol is important. Guests who are relaxing and enjoying food may not be drinking as much or as quickly. In general, food slows the absorption of alcohol into the small intestine. This delay gives the liver more time to break down the alcohol in the person's blood. Food also helps protect the stomach from alcohol irritation. The foods that work best at slowing alcohol absorption are fatty, high-protein foods. Following are some of the foods that help slow alcohol's absorption:

beef tacos	cheese	chicken wings
crackers and dip	fried foods	meat balls
pizza		

Sugars and **carbohydrates** (starches) digest quickly and do not help slow the absorption of alcohol into the bloodstream—they actually can speed alcohol's absorption. Also, very salty foods stimulate thirst and can lead a guest to drink more beverage alcohol.

Water

Water dilutes alcohol and relieves thirst. Water should be served with **all** beverage alcohol.

Carbonation

Carbonation speeds alcohol's absorption. Sparkling wines and drinks mixed with carbonated liquids, such as soda or tonic, pass through the stomach and enter the small intestine where they will quickly be absorbed into the bloodstream.

Body Size, Fat-to-Muscle Ratio, and Gender

A person's body size, fat-to-muscle ratio, and gender greatly influence the effects of alcohol.

Body Size. A large person can consume more beverage alcohol and take a longer time to react to that alcohol in comparison with a small person.

Fat-to-Muscle Ratio. Body fat does not absorb alcohol. In a person with considerable body fat, alcohol will concentrate in his or her bloodstream. This means that if two people are the same size but have a different percentage of body fat, the person with more body fat will become intoxicated by drinking less beverage alcohol.

Gender. Women tend to become intoxicated more quickly and with less beverage alcohol than men. This is because women are generally smaller than men and have a higher percentage of body fat. Women also have less of a stomach enzyme that helps neutralize alcohol.

Amount, Time, and Weight

To monitor a guest's reaction to alcohol, observe the amount of beverage alcohol he or she consumes, the time over which he or she consumes it, and the physical size of the guest. To keep a guest's BAC below your state's legal level of intoxication, the guidelines in *Exhibit 1.2* usually apply when estimating how much beverage alcohol a guest can safely consume.

Exhibit 1.2 Guidelines for Estimating Beverage Alcohol Consumption Limits

The First Hour:
Small person: 1 to 2 drinks*
Medium person: 2 to 3 drinks
Large person: 3 to 4 drinks

Subsequent Hours:
One drink per hour for each person, regardless of body size.

*One drink = ½ ounce of pure alcohol

Exhibit 1.3 is a more detailed chart to help you evaluate how much beverage alcohol guests can safely consume.

Exhibit 1.3 Know Your Limit

Body Weight	Number of Drinks* during a two-hour period									
100 lbs.	1	2	3	4	5	6	7	8	9	10
120 lbs.	1	2	3	4	5	6	7	8	9	10
140 lbs.	1	2	3	4	5	6	7	8	9	10
160 lbs.	1	2	3	4	5	6	7	8	9	10
180 lbs.	1	2	3	4	5	6	7	8	9	10
200 lbs.	1	2	3	4	5	6	7	8	9	10
220 lbs.	1	2	3	4	5	6	7	8	9	10
240 lbs.	1	2	3	4	5	6	7	8	9	10

Be Careful Driving	Driving May Be Impaired	Do Not Drive
BAC to 0.05%	0.05–0.09%**	0.10% & Up

BAC—Blood Alcohol Concentration

* One drink is 1¼ oz. of 80-proof liquor, 12 oz. of beer, or 4-oz. of wine.

** In some states, legal intoxication may be 0.08%.

This chart provides averages only. Individuals may vary, and factors such as food in the stomach, medication, and fatigue can affect your tolerance.

Courtesy of the National Restaurant Association. Source: Distilled Spirits Council of the United States, Incorporated.

Rapid or Erratic Absorption

Certain individuals are considered high-risk when consuming beverage alcohol. These individuals can absorb alcohol more rapidly than the average person. Their alcohol absorption can be erratic, beginning slowly and then rapidly increasing. Talk to your guests as you serve them to help identify and monitor those who are high-risk.

Stress, Depression, Dieting, and Fatigue

A person who is under stress or depressed might have a strong reaction to alcohol. A temporary lining can coat the stomach to protect it from excess acid released when a person is nervous.

This protective lining also traps beverage alcohol in the stomach and prevents it from moving to the small intestine where it is absorbed into the bloodstream. As a person drinks, he or she does not feel the effect of the alcohol, and may drink more, seeking the anticipated high or feeling of relaxation. Eventually, the temporary stomach lining dissolves, and the alcohol quickly moves into the small intestine and the bloodstream causing the person's BAC to quickly rise.

A guest who is dieting may not have eaten for quite some time and it could be difficult to convince him or her to order food. Therefore, any beverage alcohol he or she consumes will be quickly absorbed into the bloodstream.

Fatigue also causes alcohol to be quickly absorbed. Fatigue can affect one's judgment and compound some of alcohol's effects.

Altitude

An altitude change can surprise unsuspecting people by affecting their absorption of alcohol. A "lowlander" vacationing at a higher altitude can discover that for the first few days of the vacation, until he or she becomes accustomed to the different atmospheric pressure, the drinks he or she usually has will seem nearly twice as strong. If you work in high altitudes, such as ski resorts, watch for strong guest reactions to beverage alcohol.

Tolerance

The human body and brain can build a tolerance to alcohol. **Tolerance** is the ability to endure the effects of alcohol without exhibiting the usual symptoms. An experienced drinker can consume a lot of beverage alcohol without feeling or showing its effects. He or she usually has learned to hide the effects, even after becoming legally intoxicated. Inexperienced drinkers, on the other hand, can show signs of intoxication before they are legally intoxicated because their bodies are unaccustomed to alcohol and sensitive to smaller amounts. Always monitor your guests to avoid overserving.

Medications

Medications, both over-the-counter and prescription, can strongly influence the effects of alcohol. Certain drugs, such as cold tablets, allergy medications, tranquilizers, high blood pressure medications, and antihistamines, depress the body's central nervous system. Alcohol can further interfere with the body's metabolism of some medications, causing the drugs to build up in the body instead of break down. These reactions magnify the impact of both the drug and the alcohol. For example, a combination of alcohol and barbiturates (sleep-inducers) or tranquilizers can be fatal.

Some guests may not realize how dangerous it is to mix a seemingly harmless over-the-counter medication with beverage alcohol. Try to be aware of guests who are taking medication. Monitor guests' drinking and observe their behavioral changes. You may have to cut off beverage alcohol service and make certain the guest does not drive after taking medication and drinking beverage alcohol.

Illegal Drugs

Illegal drugs are dangerous when mixed with alcohol. Do **not** serve a guest who appears to be under the influence of illegal drugs or allow that guest to drive away from the premises. Immediately contact your manager if you suspect illegal drug activity at your establishment.

Behavioral Signs of Alcohol Absorption

Closely watching your guests' behavior is important for safeguarding your guests, yourself, and your establishment.

Significant Behavioral Changes

People have different personalities and different ways of socializing. A change in behavior is more significant than the actual behavior itself. There is a significant difference between a loud and boisterous guest and a guest who is quiet when he or she first arrives at your establishment and then becomes loud and boisterous after a few drinks.

Observing behavioral changes also can help prevent embarrassing mistakes. Certain disabilities and physical conditions can cause a guest to stumble, slur his or her speech, or have difficulty concentrating. An unobservant server may believe that these are signs that the guest is intoxicated.

Relaxed Inhibitions. When alcohol first reaches the brain, a guest's normal inhibitions can become relaxed. A person may say or do things he or she normally would not. The following are signs of relaxed inhibitions:

♦ Becoming overly friendly to employees or other guests.

♦ Becoming detached, brooding, or quiet.

♦ Suddenly leaving a group of friends and drinking alone.

♦ Suddenly annoying other guests or using foul language.

♦ Becoming loud and making rude comments about other people.

Impaired Judgment. As a guest consumes more beverage alcohol, the brain's control of emotion and judgment is affected. The guest's ability to make sensible decisions can be hindered. He or she may not realize that in this condition it is unsafe to drive a vehicle. The following are examples of impaired judgment:

♦ Becoming angry, tearful, or extremely emotional.

♦ Complaining about the strength of a drink after having consumed others of the same strength without complaining.

♦ Drinking faster or switching to larger or stronger drinks.

♦ Making irrational or argumentative statements.

♦ Becoming careless with money, such as suddenly buying drinks for strangers.

Slowed Reaction Time. After a person consumes a considerable amount of beverage alcohol, his or her reaction time and responses become slower. The person may appear to be moving in slow motion and exhibit the following signs:

- Loss of concentration, memory, and the ability to think clearly.

- Drowsiness.

- Inability to focus eyes and loss of eye contact.

- Slurred speech.

Impaired Motor Coordination. After consuming a considerable amount of beverage alcohol, motor skills are severely affected. Signs of **ataxia**, the inability to coordinate voluntary muscle movement, including loss of balance and coordination, are present. The following signs characterize ataxia:

- Staggering or stumbling.

- Falling down or bumping into chairs.

- Inability to pick up money off a table.

- Spilling drinks.

- Dozing or swaying when seated.

Remember: Observation and good customer service are the keys to evaluating how alcohol is affecting a guest.

Chapter 1 Exercise

1. Which one of the following drinks has twice as much alcohol as the others?

   a) A 12-ounce glass of beer.

   b) An 8-ounce glass of wine.

   c) A straight (containing only alcohol) drink or a mixed drink made with 1¼ ounces of 80-proof liquor.

   d) A straight drink or a mixed drink made with 1 ounce of 100-proof liquor.

2. Most of the alcohol a person consumes is absorbed into the bloodstream from what part of the body?

   a) Mouth.

   b) Stomach.

   c) Small intestine.

   d) Liver.

3. Blood alcohol content or concentration (BAC) is the amount of:

   a) beverage alcohol a person has consumed.

   b) beverage alcohol in the stomach.

   c) alcohol in the bloodstream.

   d) blood in the bloodstream.

4. Approximately how many drinks does the liver metabolize (break down) in one hour?

   a) One drink.

   b) Two drinks.

   c) Three drinks.

   d) Four drinks.

5. Alcohol does **not** affect the body by:

    a) weakening judgment, memory, and muscle coordination.
    b) stimulating the central nervous system.
    c) causing the body to lose fluids.
    d) relaxing inhibitions.

6. Why does alcohol rapidly spread throughout the entire body once it has entered the bloodstream? Because alcohol:

    a) dissolves in water and can easily pass through cell walls.
    b) contains a high degree of acid.
    c) thickens the blood.
    d) destroys blood cells.

7. What effect does fatty, high-protein food have on the body's absorption of alcohol into the bloodstream?

    a) It slows absorption by slowing the flow of alcohol into the small intestine.
    b) It has no effect.
    c) It increases absorption by stimulating the flow of stomach acids.
    d) It slows absorption by decreasing hunger.

8. A person would be at the highest risk for becoming intoxicated if he or she:

    a) is a large, happy, muscular person in good health.
    b) is a small, depressed, dieting person with a high degree of body fat.
    c) consumes beverage alcohol every day.
    d) eats a large dinner just before consuming beverage alcohol.

9. Which one of the following statements is **true**?

   a) Alcohol and drugs are **never** harmful when used together.

   b) Alcohol and drugs can be harmful when taken together.

   c) Alcohol is often prescribed as a way to increase a drug's benefits.

   d) Drugs, especially stimulants, often lower a person's BAC.

10. What is the **most** important behavior to note when estimating a guest's alcohol consumption?

    a) Loud talking.

    b) Cursing.

    c) Changing behaviors.

    d) Brooding.

THE LAW AND YOUR RESPONSIBILITY

Test Your Responsible Beverage Alcohol Service IQ

1. **True or False:** Employees and liquor-serving establishments cannot be held responsible for a guest's actions after serving him or her beverage alcohol. (See *Introduction*, page 22.)

2. **True or False:** Less than five percent of all traffic fatalities are teenagers. (See *Helping Prevent Drunk Driving*, page 22.)

3. **True or False:** In most states, it is illegal to serve a minor beverage alcohol. (See *State Liquor Codes*, page 23.)

4. **True or False:** In most states, it is illegal to serve an intoxicated individual beverage alcohol. (See *State Liquor Codes*, page 23.)

5. **True or False:** Bartenders are the only employees who can be held liable for serving beverage alcohol to an intoxicated individual. (See *Employee Liability*, page 27.)

Learning Objectives

After completing this chapter, you should be able to:

♦ Understand the nationwide concern for responsible beverage alcohol service, especially for preventing drunk driving crashes.

♦ Comply with your state's liquor code, especially in not serving beverage alcohol to minors and intoxicated individuals.

♦ Understand your civil law responsibilities, especially the need to show reasonable care when serving beverage alcohol.

♦ Understand employee and third-party liability.

Introduction

Under the law, hospitality establishments and their employees can be held at least partially responsible for their guests' actions after serving them beverage alcohol. Knowing your state laws and following your establishment's policies, can help create a safer, more enjoyable environment for your guests.

Helping Prevent Drunk Driving

Drunk driving is a high-profile issue in almost every community. Although the number of drunk driving crashes has decreased over the past decade, drinking too much beverage alcohol is still a major cause of traffic fatalities and serious injuries. Laws governing beverage alcohol service are greatly influenced by statistics such as the following:

♦ In 1993, the National Highway Traffic Safety Administration (NHTSA) concluded that 12,379 people were killed in drunk driving crashes. Drunk driving fatalities represented 31 percent of all fatal crashes.

♦ The Traffic Injury Research Foundation determined that 93 percent of the drunk drivers killed in automobile accidents in 1991 had previous **DWI, driving while intoxicated**, or **DUI, driving under the influence**, convictions. Of those 93 percent, more than 78 percent had a BAC higher than 0.15. Forty percent of all drivers who were killed in 1991 and had been drinking, had a BAC of at least 0.20—double the legal limit of 0.10 in most states. The Research Foundation considered a drunk driver to be someone who had a BAC of 0.10 or higher.

♦ In 1993, the National Transportation Safety Board (NTSB) reported that 7.1 percent of all licensed drivers were teenagers and 14.9 percent of all traffic fatalities were teenagers. Since teenagers tend to be inexperienced drivers, those who consume beverage alcohol, which can slow a person's reflexes and reaction times, can increase their chances of being in a drunk driving crash. Many states are considering lowering the BAC that classifies teen drinkers as intoxicated.

Overall, national trends are to increase the penalties for drunk driving and place more responsibility on establishments to identify and not serve minors and intoxicated individuals.

State Liquor Codes

State liquor codes govern liquor licenses. Each area's liquor code covers a variety of regulations, but the key issue is who **not** to serve. In most areas, it is illegal to serve beverage alcohol to minors and intoxicated individuals.

Remember: You have the right to protect your guests, yourself, and your establishment. There is not a penalty for refusing to serve beverage alcohol to someone you merely suspect is a minor or an intoxicated individual.

Minors

In most states, it is illegal to serve a minor beverage alcohol. A **minor**, in reference to legal beverage alcohol service, is an individual under the age of 21. **Always** ask a guest to show a valid picture ID to establish his or her age. Preventing underage drinking can be difficult because laws vary from area to area.

◆　In some areas, it is **not** illegal for a minor to attempt to purchase beverage alcohol or to present a false ID. However, in most areas, it is illegal for you to serve or sell beverage alcohol to a minor. You can be prosecuted, even if the minor is not.

◆　In some areas, minors are legally permitted to enter bars. Nevertheless, each establishment has the right to deny entrance to all minors.

◆ In some areas, parents are permitted to offer beverage alcohol to their minor children in a bar or restaurant. Minors also may be allowed to drink beverage alcohol at a banquet or a private celebration, such as a wedding reception.

Carefully follow your establishment's policies and contact your manager if you suspect a minor is illegally consuming beverage alcohol on your premises.

My establishment's policies for serving beverage alcohol to minors are: _____
_____
_____.

Intoxicated Individuals

In most areas, it is illegal to serve an intoxicated individual beverage alcohol. This applies whether the person has been drinking at your establishment or arrived at your establishment already intoxicated. The law can hold establishments and their employees responsible for keeping:

◆ Track of how many drinks a guest has consumed and determining whether the guest can safely consume more beverage alcohol.

◆ An intoxicated individual from driving away from the establishment and calling the police if an intoxicated person drives away.

My establishment's policies for serving beverage alcohol to intoxicated individuals are: _____
_____
_____.

Pregnant Women

Currently, no state laws forbid serving beverage alcohol to pregnant women. The government requires a warning label to be on every beverage alcohol container. You may be required to post a sign, for guests to see, that warns of the effects of alcohol on the fetus.

Other Areas of Compliance with State Liquor Codes

Illegal Drugs. It is illegal to use, have, buy, or sell drugs or to act as a middleperson in a drug transaction. Any drug activity at your establishment can seriously jeopardize the safety of your guests and yourself. Immediately contact your manager if you become aware of illegal drug activity at your establishment.

Transporting Beverage Alcohol on or off Premises. In some areas, it can be illegal to bring beverage alcohol on or off your premises. Watch your guests, politely explain the law to anyone who may be breaking it, and do not let guests violate the law. Remember, guests may not know beverage alcohol laws, so be patient when explaining the laws to them.

My establishment's policies about bringing beverage alcohol on or off the premises are: _____

_____

_____.

Reasonable Care

Reasonable care refers to the standard or degree of care, precaution, or diligence expected in a particular set of circumstances, including such care as an ordinary prudent person would exercise. An establishment can be guilty of **negligence** when it fails to act with reasonable care in a situation where it has a duty to do so, and that failure causes injury. **Foreseeability** is the reasonable anticipation that a particular action will likely result in harm or injury.

When interpreting reasonable care, the courts generally have found that an establishment's duty is to do nothing to cause injury or permit injury to occur as a result of the way the establishment serves beverage alcohol or handles guests who consume beverage alcohol. This duty applies to individuals who:

◆ Purchase beverage alcohol and consume it on or off your premises.

◆ Enter your premises after having consumed beverage alcohol.

◆ Enter your premises and encounter people who have consumed beverage alcohol.

◆ Encounter, away from your establishment, people who have consumed beverage alcohol on your premises or people who have entered your establishment after consuming beverage alcohol and then been allowed to drive away.

A person aware he or she can be held liable would not serve beverage alcohol to an intoxicated individual or a minor and would not allow an intoxicated individual to drive away.

Actual or Constructive Knowledge

A person can be responsible for his or her actual and constructive knowledge. **Actual knowledge** is what a person knows in a specific set of circumstances, including the person's awareness of conditions that may violate a legal requirement. **Constructive knowledge** is what a person exercising reasonable care should know about a specific set of circumstances. These concepts help define the potential dangers of illegally serving beverage alcohol.

When applying the concepts of reasonable care and actual and constructive knowledge to the facts of a case, a court will consider factors such as whether there was a known history of similar events at the establishment and whether the event was foreseeable. For example, courts tend to hold establishments responsible for observing the:

◆ Amount of beverage alcohol a guest consumes.

- Amount of time he or she takes to consume the beverage alcohol.

- Guest's behavior, including any signs of intoxication.

- Guest's history of behavior at the establishment, if any.

- Guest's known history of excessive drinking, if any.

The following lawsuit was based on the absence of constructive knowledge and the failure to exercise reasonable care.

Case 1

A bar was ordered to pay $2.2 million to a woman injured in a drunk driving crash caused by an intoxicated individual who had been drinking at the bar. The guest was served triple scotches for over five hours although several other customers observed the guest behaving in an intoxicated manner.

Employee Liability

Servers are not the only employees that can be held liable if they fail to exercise reasonable care. A valet who hands car keys to an intoxicated guest can be held liable for any injuries the guest causes, even though the valet did not serve the guest beverage alcohol. The following case is an example of this type of liability.

Case 2

A bartender changed a flat tire for an intoxicated guest. The bartender was found liable and was successfully sued for helping put the intoxicated driver on the road, where he subsequently injured someone.

Third-Party Liability

Establishments and their employees also can be faced with **third-party liability** if they are found responsible for beverage alcohol-related deaths or injuries. Under this type of liability, an establishment or its owners, managers, and employees can be held responsible for an injury even if they did not directly cause it.

Third-party liability can apply to various injuries that an intoxicated individual causes. For example, if a person is injured by a drunk driver who was served beverage alcohol at your establishment, then you and your establishment can be held liable for the damages sustained by the person even if you or your establishment did not directly cause the injury.

In some states, the laws governing third-party liability in beverage alcohol-related cases are known as dram shop laws. The term originates from Old English laws in which taverns were referred to as dram shops. **Dram shop laws** hold liquor-serving establishments liable if they serve beverage alcohol to a guest who leaves intoxicated and then injures another person. In states without dram shop laws, the common law of negligence and the concept of reasonable care apply to liquor-serving establishments.

Benefits of Responsible Beverage Alcohol Service Policies and Training

You benefit when you help make your establishment's beverage alcohol service policies work. You safeguard your guests, your co-workers, your establishment, and yourself. You raise the quality of service you provide, satisfy your guests, and increase the amount of income you can earn. Overall, responsible beverage alcohol service policies and training make your establishment a better, safer place to work and visit.

Chapter 2 Exercise

1. Which one of the following is the national trend in laws concerning drunk driving?

   a) Raising the BAC defining intoxication to 0.12.
   b) Increasing the penalties for drunk driving.
   c) Placing less responsibility on establishments to identify and not serve minors.
   d) Raising the national drinking age to 25.

2. Which one of the following statements is **false**? In some areas:

   a) minors are penalized for attempting to purchase beverage alcohol.
   b) minors can be served past the point of intoxication if they will not be driving when they leave the premises.
   c) minors are allowed to enter bars.
   d) parents are permitted to offer beverage alcohol to their minor children in a bar or restaurant.

3. When an individual arrives at your establishment already intoxicated, what should you do?

   a) Serve the individual only one alcohol beverage.
   b) Send the individual away.
   c) Do not serve the individual any beverage alcohol and keep him or her from driving away.
   d) Give the individual coffee and send him or her away.

4. Establishments and their employees are **not** responsible for:

    a) keeping track of how many drinks a guest has consumed.

    b) charging too much for beverage alcohol.

    c) refusing to serve beverage alcohol to a suspected minor.

    d) refusing to serve beverage alcohol to a suspected intoxicated individual.

5. What should you do if you become aware of illegal drug activity at your establishment?

    a) Go undercover and investigate.

    b) Make a citizen's arrest.

    c) Take the illegal drugs as evidence and go to the police.

    d) Immediately contact your manager.

6. Under what type of liability can your establishment be sued by a person injured by a drunk driver who became intoxicated at your establishment?

    a) Third-party liability.

    b) Second-party liability.

    c) Constructive knowledge liability.

    d) Actual knowledge liability.

7. In some states, the laws governing third-party liability in beverage alcohol-related cases are known as:

    a) reasonable care liability.

    b) negligence laws.

    c) dram shop laws.

    d) hospitality laws.

8. Which one of the following statements is **false**?

    a) Negligence involves the failure to exercise reasonable care.

    b) Reasonable care refers to the standard of care expected in a particular set of circumstances.

    c) To provide reasonable care when serving beverage alcohol, an establishment must not do anything to cause injury or permit it to occur.

    d) An establishment is **never** liable if it makes an honest mistake when serving beverage alcohol.

9. A court can hold a server liable for his or her:

    a) third-party knowledge.

    b) hospitality knowledge.

    c) actual and constructive knowledge.

    d) reasonable knowledge.

10. Which one of the following statements is **true**?

    a) Employees can be held liable if they fail to exercise reasonable care.

    b) Servers and bartenders are the only employees at risk in beverage alcohol-related lawsuits.

    c) Employees can be liable only in drunk driving cases.

    d) Employees returning car keys to an intoxicated guest are not liable for that guest's actions.

TECHNIQUES FOR RESPONSIBLE BEVERAGE ALCOHOL SERVICE

Test Your Responsible Beverage Alcohol Service IQ

1. **True or False:** False IDs are always easy to detect. (See *Checking Age Identification,* page 34.)

2. **True or False:** Always ask for a second ID when a guest presents an ID without a picture. (See *Checking Age Identification,* page 34.)

3. **True or False:** When refusing beverage alcohol service or admission to minors, act judgmental and authoritative. (See *Refusing a Minor Service or Admission,* page 38.)

4. **True or False:** Always bring a guest another drink before he or she has finished the first one. (See *Standardizing Recipes and Service,* page 43.)

5. **True or False:** If a guest does not appear intoxicated, there is no need to keep track of the amount of beverage alcohol he or she consumes. (See *Counting Drinks,* page 48.)

Learning Objectives

After completing this chapter, you should be able to:

◆ Communicate with managers, co-workers, and guests to follow effective beverage alcohol service policies.

◆ Control entrance into your establishment by checking IDs.

◆ Follow procedures for standardizing recipes and service.

◆ Estimate, monitor, and control the beverage alcohol service of each guest.

Introduction

The goal of responsible beverage alcohol service is to give your guests the best possible service, protect guests' safety, protect yourself and your establishment, and obey your state's liquor code. Be sure to understand and follow your establishment's policies. Whether you work at a lounge, a banquet or party facility, a stadium or arena, a hotel, or a casino, you should learn basic beverage alcohol service skills and adapt those skills to fit the special needs of your particular establishment. Communicate with your managers and co-workers to adapt your skills and the establishment's policies to your daily responsibilities.

Communication: The Key to Making Policies Work

Communication is the key to ensuring that your establishment's policies are carefully followed. Establish communication between managers, doorstaff, valets, security staff, servers, bartenders, and any other co-workers involved in beverage alcohol service.

Communication is especially important:

♦ **At shift changes.** If you or another server has slowed or refused beverage alcohol service to a guest—or believes that these actions may become necessary—be sure to inform your manager and your co-workers on the next shift.

♦ **Between different areas in the establishment.** A guest who has been drinking in the bar can move to another area of the establishment. If you decide to slow beverage alcohol service to a guest, you need to tell your manager and your co-workers in other areas.

♦ **Between you and your guests.** Inform guests about the key points of your policies, such as a designated driver program or an alternate transportation program. (*Chapter 4* discusses preventing an intoxicated guest from driving.) Materials you may use to inform guests about beverage alcohol safety include table tents, printed napkins, and menu statements.

♦ **When serving beverage alcohol.** Good communication can help you avoid serving beverage alcohol to minors and intoxicated individuals.

♦ **When controlling admission.** Controlling admission to your establishment is the first line of defense against illegal beverage alcohol service.

Checking Age Identification

Carefully check IDs. Be sure that IDs are valid and depict the person presenting the ID. Minors frequently obtain beverage alcohol by presenting a valid ID that belongs to someone else.

Validity

Know the forms of ID that are valid in your area. In many parts of the United States, only the following IDs are considered valid:

♦ A state-issued driver's license.

♦ A state-issued ID.

♦ A military ID.

♦ A current passport.

An alien residency (green) card may be acceptable, provided the card has a photo. If a guest shows you an ID that does not have a photo, ask to see a photo ID.

Note: If your local law specifies a state-issued ID, the following IDs are **not** valid: a birth certificate, a company ID from the guest's employer, and an ID issued by a private identification company.

My establishment accepts the following IDs: _____
_____
_____.

Types of False Identification

You should be able to recognize these commonly used false IDs:

- A driver's license or ID altered to include a false picture, false dates, and other incorrect data.

- A counterfeit card created with a camera, computer, and lamination equipment.

Two types of false IDs that are hard to detect are:

- A genuine ID issued to one person but used by another.

- A genuine ID illegally obtained by presenting false information, such as a counterfeit birth certificate.

Spotting False Identification

Become familiar with the valid IDs and driver's licenses in your state and nearby states. Use reference materials that your manager provides to check the legitimacy of IDs. Take time to carefully look at IDs to make sure they are legitimate.

Birth Date. Thoroughly look at the birth date. It is one of the most commonly altered items on an ID.

Expiration Date. The ID should still be valid. All driver's licenses have expiration dates, but many state-issued IDs are indefinitely valid.

Security Pattern. The pattern or lines in the background or across the front should appear correct and unbroken. Many states now print the state name over and over, in phantom letters, across the license and photo.

State Seal. The seal should be the proper size and in the proper location. On many IDs, the seal overlaps from the printed area onto the photo. There should not be a break in the continuity of the seal at this overlap.

Color. The colored areas should be the correct color. Check the photo background color and the colors in the printed area against the colors of a valid ID.

Lamination. The clear plastic coating should be the proper thickness, without irregularities or evidence of double lamination.

Material Strength. A non-tearable driver's license should not be able to be ripped or torn. Know if your state issues non-tearable licenses. Be especially careful using this method for identifying false IDs because some states make licenses with soft materials that will tear.

Size. The license or ID should be the proper size. Forgeries can be larger or smaller than legitimate IDs.

Coding. Special color bands, number series, or phantom over-type denoting the age of the ID owner should agree with the birth date on the ID.

Signature. Check each ID for any alterations or forgery. If you think the ID is false, ask the person to sign his or her name, then compare the two signatures.

Checking Identification and the Guests Who Present Them

Many false IDs are difficult to detect. Carefully observe the person presenting the ID. Since most of your guests will present valid IDs, be pleasant to everyone while watching for false IDs. General rules for checking IDs include the following:

◆ Always smile, establish eye contact, and greet the guest before asking to see the ID.

◆ Check all guests each time they enter. A person gaining admission without showing his or her ID can pass that ID to a minor.

◆ Politely ask the guest to remove the ID from his or her wallet. Do **not** remove an ID from a guest's wallet or purse.

◆ Always check to see that the person handing you the ID is the owner of that ID. Look at the physical description on the ID, especially the height and weight. Could they match the person handing you the ID? Look at the birth date on the ID. Is it appropriate for the person handing you the ID? Does the photo appear to be the person handing you the ID?

◆ Feel the ID, checking for cuts, pinholes (bleach can be inserted through a pinhole to erase certain aspects of a date), improper lamination, and other alterations. Turn the ID over and look for changes on the back. Look for breaks in the lamination around the picture.

◆ Examine the ID with a light source behind it; a flashlight will do. Cuts, erasures, and other alterations will clearly show up when an ID is lit from the back.

◆ Ask for a second valid ID when a guest presents an ID without a picture or a state ID with which you are not familiar.

◆ Notice the guest's appearance and behavior. Minors often look young. They may act underage by avoiding eye contact with employees, appearing ill at ease or nervous, avoiding adults waiting to enter your establishment, or giggling if they are admitted or when they order drinks.

◆ Be careful when checking military IDs. Often, the person's hair is very short in the picture, but their hairstyle may have changed. Carefully look at the ID presenter's chin line, nose, and ears.

◆ If it is necessary to question the ID presenter, hold the ID and ask a few questions, such as the following:

- "What is your address?"

- "What is your social security number?"

- "What is your middle name?"

- "When were you born?"

- "What is your astrological sign?"

- "How do you spell your last name?"

A guest's uncertainty or hesitation when answering any of these questions should make you suspicious. Have a pen and paper ready to ask the guest to sign his or her name. Compare that signature with the one on the ID. They should match.

Using a Video Camera at the ID-Checking Station

A video recording can help determine whether an individual entered your establishment and had his or her ID carefully checked. If your establishment has a video camera at the entrance, position yourself so the camera can record the face of the person presenting the ID, the ID being checked, and you checking the ID. A clock and a calendar should also be at the entrance to establish the date and time.

Refusing a Minor Service or Admission

When you must refuse beverage alcohol service or admission to a minor, always express regret and never sound judgmental or authoritative. Be firm, but do not embarrass the minor.

> **Correct:** "I'm sorry, but I can't let you in without a valid ID. That's our policy."

> **Incorrect:** "You haven't got an ID, kid? Forget it, you can't come in."

Communicate your decision to refuse entrance or beverage alcohol service to a minor to co-workers. Other rules that your establishment may enforce are:

♦ A minor may not be allowed in the bar but can be served food and non-alcohol beverages in the restaurant.

♦ If a minor is in the restaurant with guests over 21, the minor can be served non-alcohol beverages and food. Observe the table to make sure other guests do not serve the minor beverage alcohol. If this occurs, contact a manager. If the guests continue to give the minor beverage alcohol, you will have to stop beverage alcohol service to the table.

Confiscating Identification

Follow your establishment's policies if you suspect someone has shown you a false, altered, or stolen ID.

You should know and record your establishment's policies regarding the following:

♦ When you should confiscate an ID.

♦ Who has the authority to confiscate an ID.

♦ How to handle a person presenting a false ID.

♦ What to do with a confiscated ID.

My establishment's policies for confiscating IDs are: _____
_____
_____.

When an ID is confiscated or a minor is turned over to the authorities, immediately fill out an incident report. Thoroughly record all details. (See *Completing an Incident Report* in *Chapter 4*.)

Adapt Your Skills to Your Establishment

Lounges, banquet and party facilities, stadiums and arenas, hotels, and casinos face their own challenges for responsibly serving beverage alcohol. After learning the basic responsible beverage alcohol service skills in this chapter, apply them to your establishment's needs.

Lounges

Most guests come to lounges to enjoy the atmosphere and beverage alcohol. This often puts lounges in the spotlight for law enforcement. You and your co-workers must be especially careful to avoid serving beverage alcohol to minors and intoxicated individuals.

Doorstaff. Doorstaff should be gracious and pleasant, not intimidating. Be consistent, reasonable, and pleasant—this will help you deal with troublesome guests and earn the other guests' support.

Entrances. Have enough help at entrances to ensure quick entry and that every ID is carefully checked. Know who to call if a large group unexpectedly arrives.

Law Enforcement. Always inform a manager if the police arrive. Allow police to immediately enter your establishment.

Banquets and Parties

Businesses that cater to banquets and large parties face unique challenges. Consider the wedding reception at which the bride is 20 years old and wants to have champagne on her wedding day, the retirement party with an open bar at which the guest of honor continues to celebrate past the point of good judgment, and the banquet in a large hotel where the guests can move into one of three different lounges, ordering drinks in each one.

Working with the Host. When the party is being booked, the host should be informed that your establishment complies with the law and will not serve beverage alcohol to minors or intoxicated individuals. The host also should be informed about your policies to slow beverage alcohol service to guests who begin to show signs of intoxication. Ask your manager how to work with the host if any problems arise during the event.

Minors. Plan ahead if you know minors will be present. Carefully check IDs and find out from your manager if the host told the minors that they would not be served beverage alcohol. Politely offer minors non-alcohol beverages. Consider using one kind of glass for minors and another for guests drinking beverage alcohol.

Servers. Remember that guests may be moving around, so counting drinks will be difficult. Concentrate on guests' behavioral changes. Be alert and prepared to respond to a minor who switches glasses with a friend or has been served a drink by a friend or family member. Communicate with your co-workers, especially during shift changes.

Stadiums and Arenas

Service Policies. Special policies, procedures, and planning can help you safely and responsibly serve beverage alcohol to large groups. Your establishment may decide to take the following types of precautions:

♦ Not to serve beer in oversized cups.

♦ Stop selling beverage alcohol well before the end of the event. For example, stop serving beverage alcohol three-quarters of the way through a game.

♦ Limit patrons to purchasing two beers at a time.

♦ Set up booths where designated drivers can sign up, put on a visible arm band or bracelet, and receive coupons for free soft drinks or non-alcohol beer. A **designated driver** decides to be responsible for driving one or more individuals who have been drinking beverage alcohol.

♦ Not to allow spectators to bring their own beverage alcohol on the premises. At the main gate, and again at the ticket gate, politely warn spectators that beverage alcohol brought on the premises will be confiscated.

Hotels

Service Policies. Know your policies for handling situations when guests are:

♦ Taking beverage alcohol back to their rooms where employees will not have control over the amount consumed.

♦ Requesting beverage alcohol from room service. Employees do not know how many people will be drinking or how much beverage alcohol they will consume.

♦ Sharing beverage alcohol in their rooms with minors.

♦ Abusing the in-room liquor supply.

♦ Assuming it is acceptable to drink heavily in the lounge or restaurant since they will be walking, not driving, to their rooms.

Immediately contact management or security when you notice a problem.

Casinos

Laws regarding beverage alcohol service in casinos vary from area to area. Some casinos offer free beverages, alcohol and non-alcohol, to their gambling guests. Monitoring guests' beverage alcohol consumption is difficult since guests usually wander around the casino. All employees should be trained in responsible beverage alcohol service and be aware that communication between employees is especially important. Special service and admittance controls, employee communication, and employee training can help you safely serve beverage alcohol in a casino.

Service Policies. Your establishment may develop the following responsible beverage alcohol service policies:

♦ Cocktails should not contain more than ⅞ oz. of 80-proof liquor when beverage alcohol is free.

♦ Serve few or no: 1) straight drinks; 2) drinks with 100-proof liquor.

♦ Standardize beer to 12 oz. servings and wine to 4 oz. servings.

♦ Carefully check IDs and admit only those guests who are 21 or older.

♦ Not admit any guest carrying a beverage.

Off-Premises Drinking of Packaged Goods

If your establishment sells packaged beverage alcohol, be sure you know your state laws concerning off-premises beverage alcohol consumption of packaged goods. Remember, like with all beverage alcohol sales, always carefully check IDs.

My establishment's policies about packaged beverage alcohol are: _____

_____

_____.

Standardizing Recipes and Service

Standardizing recipes, amounts of beverage alcohol per drink, glassware, service procedures, and last call policies establish a strong foundation for responsible beverage alcohol service and consistent profits.

Standardized Recipes

Carefully follow your establishment's recipes. All employees should make each drink the same way, with exactly the same amount of beverage alcohol. A guest should not be able to tell when different bartenders are making the drinks.

Automatic Pouring Devices

If your establishment has **automatic pouring devices** that dispense an exact amount of beverage alcohol, know how to correctly use them (see *Exhibit 3.1*). When pouring devices cannot be used, use a measuring jigger or dispense beverage alcohol in specific-sized glasses. Do **not** free pour. **Free pouring**, when beverage alcohol is dispensed without being measured, risks serving a guest too much beverage alcohol and can waste money and beverage alcohol.

Glassware

Standardized glassware can be another way of regulating the amount of beverage alcohol served. For example, a 4 ounce glass of wine is one serving. If your establishment uses 6 to 8 ounce glasses, be sure to count each glass of wine as one-and-a-half or two drinks, or fill each glass only to a specified level.

Standardized glasses also should be used for non-alcohol beverages. This precaution is particularly helpful in large group situations, such as college bars and banquets, where it is likely that underage guests will be present. Remember to be alert for guests who give beverage alcohol to minors.

Exhibit 3.1 Automatic Pouring Device

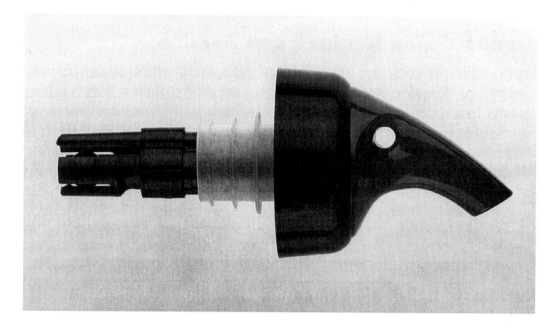

Posi-Pour 2000 photo courtesy of Magnuson Industries, Incorporated, Rockford, Illinois.

Upselling

Upselling, or **upgrading**, means offering a guest a **call** or **premium brand** of beer, wine, or spirits instead of a less expensive **well** or **house brand**. When you first approach a table, suggest specialty cocktails, particularly those that may be low in alcohol content or without alcohol.

Distilled Liquors. When a guest orders a gin and tonic, mention a few call or premium brands, such as Bombay or Tanqueray. Offer a premium scotch, such as Dewar's or Glenfiddich, when a guest orders a scotch on the rocks. Suggest a premium tequila, such as Jose Quervo or Mescal, to a guest who orders a margarita.

Wine. Upsell orders for glasses or carafes of house wine to glasses or bottles of premium wine. For example:

◆ "May I suggest Chardonnay California? It's a very dry vintage, with vanilla and oak flavors."

◆ "Yes, we do serve red wine by the glass. I recommend Vineyard's Cabernet Sauvignon, which is a robust, full-bodied red wine with a strong oak and tannin finish."

Offering Liqueurs, Cordials, and Hot Drinks. Learn when to offer a liqueur, a cordial, and a hot drink. Many, but not all, liqueurs and cordials are lower in alcohol content than whiskeys, which are 40 percent alcohol. Liqueurs and cordials are served straight up and often slowly sipped, so your guest is drinking a low-alcohol beverage at a slower rate. Become familiar with the alcohol content of all the drinks you serve (see *Appendix: Alcohol Content in Common Drinks*). As with any drink, serve water on the side.

Hot drinks, such as Irish coffee, are not necessarily lower in alcohol content, but they are usually sipped more slowly over a longer time period. The liver then has time to break down the alcohol before a guest leaves your establishment.

Service Standards

Other responsible beverage alcohol service policies include the following:

◆ Try to keep guests from urging one another to drink excessively. If a guest does not want another drink, do **not** serve him or her beverage alcohol at another guest's request. In these situations, offer food or low- or non-alcohol beverages to keep guests from being pressured to drink.

◆ **Never** stack drinks. Wait until a guest finishes the present drink before serving the next one.

Food Service

Food plays an important role in responsible beverage alcohol service. Alcohol initially tends to increase a guest's appetite, so he or she may appreciate having food available. Serving food also is an excellent way to increase sales and tips. Most importantly for beverage alcohol service, fatty, high-protein food slows the absorption of alcohol into the bloodstream.

Make suggestive selling a natural part of your food service. Practice describing food in concise, appetizing, and accurate terms.

◆ Say more than "Help yourself to our buffet," "Our special tonight is nachos," or "Can I bring you anything to eat?"

◆ Give full descriptions that will tantalize a guest and close a sale. For example, "Tonight we're featuring two new items on our buffet, bite-sized pizza with tangy sundried tomatoes and creamy mozzarella, and my favorite, hot and spicy Cajun chicken wings."

◆ If you have a free buffet or snack bar, bring guests samples, invite them to help themselves, or offer to escort them through the buffet.

Last Call

Carefully follow your establishment's policies for last call. Your goal is to allow guests time to metabolize the beverage alcohol they have consumed before they must leave your establishment. Your establishment may set up policies, such as:

◆ Scheduling last call well before closing. An hour before closing is recommended.

◆ Stopping the service of drinks that are the equivalent of two or more alcohol servings, such as Long Island iced teas or martinis, as early as an hour before last call.

◆ Combining last call with other promotional ideas, such as offering free non-alcohol beverages, cold sandwiches, or pizza.

→ My establishment's last call procedures are: _____
_____
_____ .

Make Guests Aware of Your Programs

Help remind guests to responsibly drink beverage alcohol.

◆ Use **point-of-sale (POS) materials** to emphasize beverage alcohol safety. These include table tents, buttons for you to wear, slogans on cocktail napkins and coasters, and statements on menus.

◆ Be able to explain your establishment's policies on serving beverage alcohol to minors and intoxicated individuals.

◆ Make guests aware of your designated driver or alternate transportation programs.

Evaluating Guests by the SIR Method

SIR means to Size up, Interview, and Rate a guest. Warmly greet each guest and start a conversation. Besides being hospitable, you gain a sense of the guest's personality, mental attitude, and level of beverage alcohol intake.

S: Size Up

◆ Note the guest's size and body type. Remember, a larger person can generally safely drink more beverage alcohol than a smaller person and a person with a lower percentage of body fat can generally safely drink more beverage alcohol than a person of the same size with more body fat.

I: Interview

◆ Observe behavioral signs and notice any behavioral changes.

• Talk to the guest. Was the guest previously drinking? Has the guest eaten recently or made plans to eat soon? What is the guest's mental attitude? Is the guest stressed? Happy? Upset?

• Observe the guest's general physical appearance. Is there any indication that the guest has been ill and may be taking medication? Does the guest look tired?

- Look at the guest's eyes. Are they clear? Glassy? Unfocused?

- Watch how the guest moves. How are the guest's major motor skills, such as walking or speaking, and finer motor skills, such as picking up change or lighting a cigarette?

- Listen to the guest. Is the guest's speech clear? Slurred? Irrational?

R: Rate

◆ Rate the guest's beverage alcohol consumption level as green, yellow, or red. (See *Traffic Light System* later in this chapter.)

◆ Guests who arrive at your establishment at the red level of intoxication should **not** be served any beverage alcohol.

Counting Drinks

While observing a guest's behavior and watching for significant behavioral changes, try to keep track of the amount of beverage alcohol each guest consumes. Even if a guest does not appear to be intoxicated, it is important for you to know how much beverage alcohol a guest has consumed.

◆ Since all drinks do not contain the same amount of alcohol, know or have a list of the alcohol content of each drink your establishment serves (see *Appendix*). Remember, count drinks with double amounts of alcohol, such as martinis, as two drinks.

◆ Use your establishment's system for keeping track of how many drinks a guest consumes. Notice when a guest consumes each drink. The following are examples of drink counting systems your establishment may use:

- Guest check and running tab notation. Use the back of the guest check or tab to note each drink and possibly the time it was served.

- Service bar charts. Indicate on a chart at the service bar what drink orders you have picked up.

- Seating charts. On your tray, keep charts of table and chair arrangements and mark the charts as you serve guests.

In some situations, counting drinks can be difficult, if not impossible. For example, servers at banquets, stadiums, and casinos have unique problems when attempting to count drinks because guests move around and can be served at many locations. If counting drinks will not work, you must rely on your skills to recognize the signs of intoxication.

Traffic Light System

Many establishments use a beverage alcohol consumption system based on the **traffic light system**. **Green** means safely go ahead. A guest at the green level has had little or nothing to drink and can safely be served beverage alcohol. **Yellow** calls for caution. A guest at the yellow level has begun to show the effects of beverage alcohol consumption, and service must be slowed to prevent him or her from getting to the red level. **Red** means **STOP**. The guest already has consumed too much beverage alcohol, and beverage alcohol service must immediately be stopped.

Monitoring Guests

To make good use of the Traffic Light System, monitor your guests. There are two steps to effectively monitoring guests: 1) evaluate a guest's ability to safely consume beverage alcohol; and 2) count the drinks he or she consumes.

Remember: Never serve a guest into the red level.

Green

Guests at the green level have not had anything to drink or have consumed what they easily can tolerate. Overall, guests behave sociably as if they have not been drinking. The guest seems:

♦ Relaxed.

♦ Comfortable.

♦ Talkative.

♦ Happy.

Yellow

Moving into the yellow level, a guest can become argumentative, quieter, or more talkative, depending on the individual. In the yellow level, the guest can show signs of:

♦ Reduced inhibitions.

♦ Impaired judgment.

♦ Talking or laughing louder than normal.

♦ Being overly friendly to employees and other guests.

♦ Becoming giddy—the life of the party.

♦ Arguing or baiting.

♦ Increasing use of foul language.

♦ Increasing beverage alcohol consumption.

♦ Buying rounds for strangers.

♦ Becoming careless with money.

Red

Moving into the red level, a guest reacts slowly and is less coordinated. The guest seems to be:

♦ Moving in slow motion.

- Needing time to respond to questions.

- Glassy-eyed.

- Losing his or her train of thought.

- Making irrational statements.

- Spilling drinks.

- Dropping money.

- Walking awkwardly.

- Stumbling or falling down.

- Unable to sit up straight.

Providing the Right Beverage Alcohol Service for Each Guest

Serve your guests according to their levels of consumption.

Green Level

Guests at the green level have not had anything to drink or have consumed what they easily can tolerate. These guests are usually sociable and do not act intoxicated.

Serving a guest at the green level is actually a matter of offering hospitable customer service.

- Welcome the guests. Offer them beverage alcohol, food, and other beverages. Practice suggestive selling and upselling techniques.

- Start tracking time and counting drinks when you serve the first round of beverage alcohol.

- Suggest high-protein food to slow a guest's approach to the yellow level. If free snacks are available, serve a small plate of samples.

Yellow Level

The objective at the yellow level is to ensure that guests do not reach the red level. Slow beverage alcohol service to one drink per hour, but do not avoid the guest. The guest may simply be having a good time and will slow his or her beverage alcohol consumption. You can help by using the following appropriate techniques:

♦ Continue to offer high-protein food. Use free snacks and suggestive selling to encourage consumption of food so time elapses and the liver metabolizes some of the alcohol in the guest's system.

♦ Constantly serve water.

♦ Delay service. Take time clearing used glasses and bringing fresh drinks. Do not clear and serve in one trip as you might normally do for efficiency. Change the ashtrays, replace used napkins, and wipe the table.

♦ If a guest is drinking mixed drinks and is drinking more quickly than his or her companions, offer a complimentary splash. A **complimentary splash** is a small amount of liquor with fresh ice and filler, compliments of the house. This technique buys time, gives the guest the feeling of getting a free drink, and leaves him or her with a full glass.

Occasionally, a guest will not cooperate with slowed beverage alcohol service. If you cannot discreetly convince a guest to slow or stop drinking, pass the buck. Make it someone else's fault or the fault of the establishment that service had to be slowed. For example:

"I'm sorry, it's against our policy for me to bring you another drink at this time. But, I'd be happy to bring you a soft drink. May I suggest an appetizer? Our fried cheese is excellent."

Red Level

Guests at the red level are intoxicated. Service of all beverage alcohol stops. It is **illegal** to serve an individual who is intoxicated.

Chapter 3 Exercise

1. Which one of the following is **not** a valid form of ID?

   a) State-issued driver's license.
   b) State-issued ID.
   c) Military ID.
   d) Birth certificate.

2. When checking IDs, the best procedure is to check:

   a) guests who appear to be intoxicated.
   b) guests who are clearly younger than 21.
   c) all guests IDs each time they enter.
   d) all guests IDs except those you personally know.

3. What should doorstaff do when checking IDs?

   a) Be reasonable, friendly, and consistent.
   b) Act stern and intimidating.
   c) Take IDs out of guests' wallets.
   d) Ask each guest to sign his or her name.

4. When you have to refuse entrance to a minor, what should you say?

   a) "Forget it. No ID, no admission."
   b) "I'm sorry, but I can't let you in without a valid ID."
   c) "Please leave immediately, or I'll be forced to call the police."
   d) "Sorry, man. If it was up to me, you could come in."

5. If you are serving beverage alcohol at a banquet or party, you should:

   a) focus on your job and ignore your co-workers.
   b) carefully observe guests' behavioral changes.
   c) serve beverage alcohol to a guest who may be a minor.
   d) rely on counting drinks to determine the amount of beverage alcohol a guest has consumed.

6. To consistently serve beverage alcohol, you should:
   a) standardize drink recipes.
   b) serve **all** drinks in the same type of glassware.
   c) free pour to save time.
   d) always announce last call when there are five or fewer guests left in the establishment.

7. Upselling or upgrading means:
   a) telling a guest you do not have any inexpensive beverages.
   b) raising the price of drinks on a regular basis.
   c) increasing your marketing and advertising efforts.
   d) offering a guest a call or premium brand of beverage alcohol.

8. When a guest has almost finished his or her present drink, what should you do?
   a) Bring the guest another drink without being asked.
   b) Bring another round for the whole table without being asked.
   c) Wait until he or she has finished the present drink before offering another.
   d) Say "Drink up and I'll get you another."

9. Your objective when serving guests in the yellow level is to:
   a) prevent them from reaching the red level.
   b) continue beverage alcohol service at the same rate.
   c) cut off beverage alcohol service.
   d) arrange alternate transportation.

10. How should you handle a guest in the red level?
    a) Continue beverage alcohol service at the same rate.
    b) Serve him or her only one more drink.
    c) Stop beverage alcohol service.
    d) Ask him or her to leave the establishment at once.

SERVICE IN DIFFICULT SITUATIONS

Test Your Responsible Beverage Alcohol Service IQ

1. **True or False:** Intervention is the process of discontinuing beverage alcohol service to guests in the red level. (See *Handling Difficult Situations*, page 56.)

2. **True or False:** If an intoxicated guest becomes verbally abusive or hostile, physically restrain the guest until the police arrive. (See *Handling Beverage Alcohol-Related Verbal Abuse and Violence*, page 58.)

3. **True or False:** If an intoxicated guest drives away from your establishment, call the police. (See *Ensuring Automobile Safety for Your Guests*, page 59.)

4. **True or False:** A designated driver promises not to consume any beverage alcohol. (See *Ensuring Automobile Safety for Your Guests*, page 59.)

5. **True or False:** An incident report should be filled out within a week after an incident occurs. (See *Completing an Incident Report*, page 61.)

Learning Objectives

After completing this chapter, you should be able to:

◆ Intervene as needed to discontinue beverage alcohol service and handle abusive and violent guests.

◆ Tactfully explain to a guest the need to cut off beverage alcohol service.

◆ Help ensure guests' safety by offering and arranging alternate transportation.

◆ Thoroughly document any beverage alcohol-related incident.

Introduction

When a beverage alcohol-related incident occurs, you may have to make decisions during difficult circumstances. It is important that you know your establishment's policies on handling verbal abuse and violence and preventing an intoxicated guest from driving away from your establishment. You also should know when to select alternate transportation and how to complete an incident report.

Handling Difficult Situations

Intervention is the process of discontinuing beverage alcohol service to guests in the red level. Follow your establishment's policies and involve your manager as required when carefully making the important decisions described below.

1. Who Decides to Intervene?

You may be the first to notice that a guest is intoxicated. When deciding if a guest is intoxicated, it is a good idea to ask a co-worker for a second opinion.

2. Who Intervenes?

Some establishments allow a server to handle this task while others require that a manager handle it. The person who intervenes should have a backup in case the guest becomes verbally or physically abusive. If you have the authority to discontinue beverage alcohol service, always keep your manager informed of your decision and action. Beverage alcohol service to a guest should **never** be stopped without a manager being aware of the situation.

3. How Should the Intervention Be Handled?

◆ Wait until the guest orders before refusing beverage alcohol service. If a guest has a drink and is content, the best practice is to wait. Do not antagonize the guest by announcing that "This is your last drink for tonight." Politeness is good service and a way to avoid upsetting the guest.

◆ Alert a backup. Have an experienced staff member's support if you decide to discontinue beverage alcohol service. The backup employee should stand near, but not approach, the guest. Being confronted by two or more people can intimidate a guest.

◆ If possible, isolate the guest from other guests to avoid embarrassing him or her, but make sure help is near. The pretense of a telephone call is a good way to separate a guest from his or her party. In some cases, it may be better for you to speak with the guest near an entrance, where help from the doorstaff is available and where the guest can easily be removed from the establishment if trouble occurs. If the guest refuses to leave the table, discreetly inform the guest that you will no longer serve him or her beverage alcohol.

◆ Tactfully lead into the message. Practice interventions, such as "Good evening, sir. My name is Pat. Are you enjoying yourself this evening?" Then continue, "I'm sorry, but our policy doesn't allow me to serve you more beverage alcohol. May I bring you a non-alcohol beverage or some appetizers?"

◆ Avoid being judgmental. Avoid criticizing or condemning the guest for drinking too much. **Never** accuse the guest of being drunk. Expressing concern is a good way to achieve empathy with a guest. He or she may feel understood and that you really care about his or her welfare and safety.

◆ Enlist help. If there are other people at the table, ask them to help their friend by not serving him or her beverage alcohol. For this approach, try to identify the most responsible person at the table.

◆ Be firm. Do not change your mind about discontinuing beverage alcohol service. This can allow the guest an opportunity to bargain for "just one more." Rely on your manager for support.

◆ Be patient and remain calm. Simply and clearly repeat the decision to discontinue beverage alcohol service to the guest as often as necessary.

My establishment's specific intervention policies are: _____
_____
_____
_____.

Handling Beverage Alcohol-Related Verbal Abuse and Violence

In most states, the law requires an establishment to make a reasonable effort to anticipate problems and protect guests and employees from injury.

If an intoxicated guest becomes verbally abusive or hostile, get a manager. However, if fighting or violence seems likely or occurs, immediately take the following steps:

1. Call the police. Do not assume that the situation will resolve itself—act to protect your guests, your co-workers, and yourself.

2. Try to separate the intoxicated guest from other guests.

3. Speak firmly and calmly. Repeat yourself as often as necessary to make the guest understand you.

4. Negotiate with a guest who is in the late stages of the yellow level or in the red level not to leave the establishment and to calmly wait for the police to arrive.

Caution: **Never** touch or try to physically restrain an intoxicated guest.

Ensuring Automobile Safety for Your Guests

Establishments often provide alternate transportation, a designated driver program, and procedures to prevent an intoxicated guest from getting behind the wheel. Carefully follow your establishment's policies.

Preventing an Intoxicated Guest from Driving

1. Select Alternate Transportation.

   • Decide which alternate transportation is most appropriate—whether that is calling a cab or a member of the guest's family—and insist on it.

2. Convince the Guest Not to Drive.

   • Convince the guest that you are concerned about his or her welfare and safety.

   • If the parking valet has the guest's car keys, he or she should keep them from the guest.

   • If the guest will give you the car keys, take them, tag them, and lock them away.

   • If the guest will not give you the car keys and insists on driving, warn the guest that you will call the police if he or she drives away.

   • If the guest drives away, do not attempt to use physical force to stop him or her. Call the police and give them a description of the guest and the guest's car, including its make, model, color, and license plate number.

   • If a guest is difficult and demands his or her car keys, call the police and give the keys to them when they arrive.

Alternate Transportation

When you send a guest home using alternate transportation, secure the guest's car. Have the guest take his or her personal belongings. Be sure the guest is appropriately dressed for the weather since alcohol causes the body to lose heat.

◆ If the guest takes a cab, return the guest's car keys as he or she gets into the cab.

◆ If the intoxicated guest is with a sober spouse or friend, the sober person may be able to drive the intoxicated guest home. If the guest is alone, attempt to telephone a friend or relative.

Note: Be sure to offer alternate transportation to other guests who, for reasons other than drinking, feel that they cannot safely drive. Offering this service to everyone helps remove the stigma of needing a ride.

My establishment's alternate transportation policies include:

_____

_____

_____

_____ .

Designated Driver Program

A designated driver program can help encourage the driver of a group of guests to remain sober. In this type of program, one person is the designated driver who promises not to consume any beverage alcohol. As an incentive for not drinking beverage alcohol, some establishments offer designated drivers free non-alcohol beverages or food. Some establishments also give the designated driver a coupon for a complimentary alcohol beverage the next time he or she is in and is not a designated driver.

A designated driver program can be an effective part of responsible beverage alcohol service, but it must be carefully planned and executed. Be sure to do the following:

Identify Each Designated Driver. When a group arrives, record the designated driver's name in a log. A record of designated drivers documents your actions.

Make Your Policies Clear. Be sure the driver understands that to receive complimentary non-alcohol beverages he or she cannot consume any beverage alcohol. Make it clear that he or she will receive a tab for previously free drinks if the driver reneges on the agreement. Some establishments will not serve beverage alcohol to a designated driver who no longer wishes to uphold his or her part of the agreement.

Keep Each Shift of Servers Informed. Always know who at the table or bar is not drinking beverage alcohol. Some establishments have special buttons, cards, arm bands, or badges for the designated driver. If a guest refuses a highly obvious designation, such as a badge, find an alternative the guest will accept.

Keep the Whole Group Sober. Do **not** allow other members of the group to become intoxicated—the program should not enable other guests to drink too much.

Completing an Incident Report

It is important to use an incident report to document your efforts of responsible beverage alcohol service. The incident report documents the facts of an incident and explains why certain actions were taken (see *Exhibit 4.1*).

Writing the Report

Write the report **immediately** after an incident occurs, while events and persons are clear in your mind. Do **not** wait until the end of a shift or the next day.

Always include basic information, such as the date, time, server on duty, server's station, and manager on duty. Detail as much information as possible about the incident. Include the names of guests and employees who witnessed the incident and physical descriptions of all intoxicated guests involved.

The following incidents **always** should be documented:

◆ **When Beverage Alcohol Service Is Refused.** Explain in detail the guest's behavior and why beverage alcohol service was refused. Typically, this incident occurs when a guest shows signs of intoxication.

♦ **When Transportation Is Arranged.** Note the type of transportation arranged and why you decided to use alternate transportation. Note that the guest took all of his or her personal belongings.

♦ **When a Minor Presents a False ID.** Note whether the ID was confiscated and whether it was given to the police. State if the minor was denied admission into your establishment and that beverage alcohol service was refused. Also, record if the police were notified to handle the situation.

♦ **When Police or Regulatory Agents Are Called or Visit Your Establishment.** Note the reason for the call or visit and completely describe the incident. Record who spoke with the police officer or regulatory agent, what information was provided, and the next step in the investigation process. **Always** call the police when violence occurs and when an intoxicated person drives away from your establishment.

♦ **When a Guest Has a Beverage Alcohol-Related Accident or Becomes Ill.** Record the nature of the accident or illness and the guest's symptoms. Include the aid you provided, what medical service you called, when you made the call, when the service arrived, and what treatment they provided.

Exhibit 4.1 Incident Report Form

REFUSAL OF SERVICE REPORT

LOCATION _____ DATE _____
REPORT WRITTEN BY _____ TIME _____

NAME OF PATRON _____
ADDRESS _____
CITY/STATE _____
DESCRIPTION/OBSERVATION OF PATRON _____
_____

SERVERS ON DUTY _____   _____

MANAGER ON DUTY _____
SERVICE REFUSED BY _____ TIME _____
BAR TAB   YES NO   (COPY AND ATTACH TO REPORT)

PHYSICAL DESCRIPTION REPORT

SEX	RACE	HEIGHT	WEIGHT	AGE

HAIR

EYES

GLASSES TYPE

TATTOOS

SCARS/MARKS

COMPLEXION

HAT

TIE

COAT

SHIRT

TROUSERS

SHOES

AUTOMOBILE (LICENSE NUMBER, MAKE, COLOR)

OBSERVATIONS
DESCRIBE TYPE AND COLOR OF CLOTHES: _____
_____

CONDITION OF CLOTHES: ☐ DISORDERLY ☐ DISARRANGED ☐ SOILED
☐ MUSSED ☐ ORDERLY
BREATH (ALCOHOL ODOR): ☐ STRONG ☐ MODERATE ☐ FAINT ☐ NONE
ATTITUDE: ☐ POLITE ☐ HILARIOUS ☐ TALKATIVE ☐ CAREFREE ☐ SLEEPY
☐ COCKY ☐ COMBATIVE ☐ INDIFFERENT ☐ INSULTING
☐ PROFANE ☐ COOPERATIVE
UNUSUAL ACTION: ☐ BELCHING ☐ VOMITING ☐ FIGHTING ☐ CRYING
☐ LAUGHING ☐ HICCOUGHING
SPEECH: ☐ NOT UNDERSTANDABLE ☐ MUMBLED ☐ SLURRED ☐ CONFUSED
☐ MUSH-MOUTHED ☐ THICK-TONGUED ☐ ACCENT ☐ FAIR
☐ GOOD ☐ SPEECH IMPEDIMENT
EYES: ☐ BLOODSHOT ☐ WATERY ☐ GLASSY
COMPLEXION: ☐ FLUSHED ☐ PALE ☐ OTHER
INDICATE OTHER UNUSUAL ACTIONS OR STATEMENTS, INCLUDING WHEN
FIRST OBSERVED: _____

CHECK STEPS TAKEN
___ OFFERED NON-ALCOHOLIC
        BEVERAGES
___ OFFERED FOOD
___ OFFERED TO CALL ANOTHER
        PARTY
___ SUGGESTED/CALLED A CAB

**PATRON'S ACTIONS &
COMMENTS:**
_____
_____
_____
_____

WAS PATRON ALONE? YES NO
DID PATRON DRIVE? YES NO

THE FACTS RECORDED ABOVE ARE TRUE AND ACCURATE TO THE BEST OF MY KNOWLEDGE.

SIGNATURE _____ SUPERVISOR _____ DATE _____

Reprinted with permission from the National Restaurant Association.

Chapter 4 Exercise

1. If you have to discontinue beverage alcohol service to a guest, which one of the following should you do?

    a) Alert a backup about your decision, but speak to the guest by yourself.

    b) Speak to the guest with at least two other co-workers.

    c) Send one of the doorstaff to tell the guest that beverage alcohol service has been cut off.

    d) Ignore the guest until he or she leaves.

2. What should you say to a guest when you are discontinuing beverage alcohol service?

    a) "I'm afraid you're drunk and we can't serve you any more beverage alcohol."

    b) "It's against the law to serve someone who is intoxicated, which you seem to be."

    c) "I'm sorry, but our policies don't allow me to serve you any more beverage alcohol."

    d) "Your beverage alcohol service is cut off. Please immediately leave the premises."

3. If an intoxicated guest becomes verbally abusive:

    a) ignore the situation.

    b) wait for other guests to notice before doing anything.

    c) attempt to physically restrain the guest.

    d) get a manager.

4. If fighting or violence seems likely or occurs, you should immediately:

    a) leave the room.

    b) alert a manager and call the police.

    c) attempt to physically restrain the guest.

    d) ignore the situation.

5. Which one of the following is **not** provided by establishments to ensure guests' automobile safety?

   a) A designated driver program.
   b) One free alcohol beverage for designated drivers.
   c) Free non-alcohol beverages and food for designated drivers.
   d) Alternate transportation.

6. To prevent an intoxicated guest from driving away from your establishment, it is important for you to:

   a) get the guest's car keys.
   b) take the guest's beverage alcohol away when he or she is not looking.
   c) call the police.
   d) get the guest's home phone number.

7. If an intoxicated guest drives away from your establishment, what should you do?

   a) Chase the guest in your own car.
   b) Immediately call the police and describe the guest and his or her car.
   c) Wait 24 hours, then report the incident.
   d) Wait 24 hours, then write out an incident report.

8. Which one of the following statements about designated driver programs is **false**?

   a) You should record each designated driver's name in a log.
   b) Always identify which guests are not drinking beverage alcohol.
   c) It is acceptable for other members of a group to become intoxicated if the designated driver stays sober.
   d) You should inform guests that you have a designated driver program.

9. When should you write an incident report?
    a) One day after the incident occurs.
    b) If a criminal charge or a lawsuit is filed.
    c) Immediately, so all details are clearly recorded.
    d) At the end of your shift, so service is not disrupted.

10. Which one of the following situations does **not** require filling out an incident report?
    a) A minor presents a false ID.
    b) An intoxicated guest needs alternate transportation arranged.
    c) A guest has a beverage alcohol-related accident or becomes ill.
    d) A minor is seated with adults who are drinking beverage alcohol.

CONCLUSION

Bar Code: Serving Alcohol Responsibly provides you with a strong foundation to responsibly serve beverage alcohol. You should feel confident to provide your guests with exceptional service and protect them and the public from intoxicated individuals. You also are helping your establishment earn a significant portion of its profits while increasing your own earnings. This training will help you and your establishment obey the laws, prevent accidents, and reduce the risk of a lawsuit.

As with any training, you need to practice your skills on the job. Regularly discuss important issues with your manager and co-workers and review your establishment's policies to keep them fresh in your mind. As you have learned, responsible beverage alcohol service involves more than policies, information, and training—it takes teamwork.

ALCOHOL CONTENT IN COMMON DRINKS*

DRINK	OZ. ALCOHOL	COUNT AS (NO. DRINKS)
BEER AND WINE		
Reduced Alcohol Beer (12 oz.)	0.28	½
Light Beer (12 oz.)	0.50	1
Imported Beer (12 oz.)	0.54	1
Beer (12 oz.)	0.54	1
Malt Liquor (12 oz.)	0.71	1½
Table Wine (5 oz.)	0.55	1
Champagne (5 oz.)	0.60	1
Fortified/Dessert Wine (5 oz.)	1.0	2
MIXED DRINKS		
Bloody Mary	0.60	1
Gin and Tonic	0.60	1
Highball	0.60	1
Irish Coffee	0.60	1
"On the Rocks"	0.60	1
Piña Colada	0.60	1
Screwdriver	0.60	1
Tom Collins	0.60	1
Whiskey Sour	0.60	1
Margarita	0.70	1½
Airline Miniature	0.70	1½
Gimlet	0.80	1½
Old-Fashioned	0.80	1½
Mint Julep	0.90	1½–2
Black Russian	1.0	2
Dry Martini	1.0	2
Manhattan	1.15	2
Rob Roy	1.15	2
Double "On the Rocks"	1.20	2–2½
Frozen Daiquiri	1.20	2–2½

* Provides estimates only. Mixed drinks are based on typical recipes using 80-proof liquor. The amount of alcohol in actual mixed drinks may vary.

Courtesy of Northwestern University Traffic Institute, Evanston, Illinois

GLOSSARY

Actual knowledge is what a person knows in a specific set of circumstances, including the person's awareness of conditions that may violate a legal requirement. (*Chapter 2*)

Alcohol, in this *Server Guide*, is the ingredient in beverage alcohol that can cause intoxication. (*Introduction*)

Ataxia is the inability to coordinate voluntary muscle movement, such as coordination and balance. (*Chapter 1*)

Automatic pouring devices dispense an exact amount of beverage alcohol. (*Chapter 3*)

Beverage alcohol, in this *Server Guide*, is what a person consumes. (*Introduction*)

Blood alcohol content or **concentration (BAC)** is the percentage of alcohol absorbed in the bloodstream. (*Chapter 1*)

Bloodstream is the blood circulating through a person's body. (*Chapter 1*)

Breathalyzers accurately measure a person's BAC by testing his or her breath. (*Chapter 1*)

Call or **premium brands** are more expensive brands of beer, wine, and spirits. (*Chapter 3*)

Capillaries are tiny blood vessels. When beverage alcohol is swallowed, small amounts of alcohol directly enter the bloodstream through capillaries in the mouth. (*Chapter 1*)

Carbohydrates are starches that are quickly digested and do **not** help slow the absorption of alcohol into the bloodstream. (*Chapter 1*)

Complimentary splash is a small amount of liquor with fresh ice and filler, compliments of the house. (*Chapter 3*)

Constructive knowledge is what a person exercising reasonable care should know about a specific set of circumstances. (*Chapter 2*)

Depressants reduce muscle or nerve activity. Alcohol is a depressant. (*Chapter 1*)

Designated drivers are responsible for driving one or more individuals who have been drinking beverage alcohol. (*Chapter 3*)

Distillation is when water is removed from alcohol to make a stronger beverage alcohol. (*Chapter 1*)

Distilled spirits or **liquors**, such as scotch, bourbon, gin, vodka, and rum, undergo the distillation process. (*Chapter 1*)

Diuretics help the body lose fluids and cause the sensation of thirst. Alcohol is a diuretic. (*Chapter 1*)

Dram shop laws hold liquor-serving establishments liable if they serve beverage alcohol to a guest who leaves intoxicated and causes injury to another person. (*Chapter 2*)

Drink, in this *Server Guide*, refers to any beverage containing the equivalent of ½ oz. of pure alcohol. (*Chapter 1*)

DUI means driving under the influence. (*Chapter 2*)

DWI means driving while intoxicated. (*Chapter 2*)

Fermentation is the process by which tiny life-forms, such as yeasts, break down molecules in berries, fruits, or grains to make beverage alcohol. (*Chapter 1*)

Foreseeability is the reasonable anticipation that a particular action will likely result in harm or injury. (*Chapter 2*)

Free pouring is when beverage alcohol is dispensed without being measured. (*Chapter 3*)

Green, in the Traffic Light System, is when a guest behaves sociably as if he or she has not been drinking. You should start to track time, count drinks, and offer food to slow a guest's approach to the yellow level. (*Chapter 3*)

Hypoglycemia is a decrease of sugar in the blood. Alcohol can cause hypoglycemia. (*Chapter 1*)

Incident reports document the facts of an incident and explain why certain actions were taken. (*Chapter 4*)

Inhibition is a mental or psychological process that restrains or suppresses a person's emotions, actions, or thoughts. (*Chapter 1*)

Intervention is the process of discontinuing beverage alcohol service to guests in the red level. (Chapter 4)

Liqueurs and cordials vary in alcohol content and can contain as much alcohol as whiskeys, which are 40 percent alcohol. (*Chapter 1*)

Micro-organisms are tiny life-forms, such as yeasts, that break down a plant's molecules and produce beverage alcohol during fermentation. (*Chapter 1*)

Minors, in reference to legal beverage alcohol service, are individuals under the age of 21. (*Chapter 2*)

Negligence is when an establishment fails to act with reasonable care in a situation where it has a duty to do so, and that failure causes injury. (*Chapter 2*)

Point-of-sale (POS) materials emphasize beverage alcohol safety. These materials include table tents, server buttons, slogans on cocktail napkins and coasters, and statements on menus. (*Chapter 3*)

Reasonable care refers to the standard or degree of care, precaution, or diligence expected in a particular set of circumstances, including such care as an ordinary prudent person would exercise. (*Chapter 2*)

Red, in the Traffic Light System, is when a guest reacts slowly and is less coordinated. You must **not** serve beverage alcohol to a guest in the red level. (*Chapter 3*)

Serving beverage alcohol responsibly means helping your guests enjoy beverage alcohol's pleasant aspects while safeguarding them from the unpleasant, and possibly dangerous, effects of drinking too much. (*Introduction*)

SIR means to Size up, Interview, and Rate a guest. SIR is a method of evaluating a guest's personality, mental attitude, and level of beverage alcohol intake. (*Chapter 3*)

Standardized recipes ensure the identical production of drinks. (*Chapter 3*)

State liquor codes govern liquor licenses. (*Chapter 2*)

Third-party liability allows a plaintiff (the victim) to hold an establishment, its owners, managers, and employees responsible for an injury even if they did not directly cause the injury. (*Chapter 2*)

Tolerance is the ability to endure the effects of alcohol without exhibiting the usual symptoms. (*Chapter 1*)

Traffic Light System is a beverage alcohol consumption system used to monitor and evaluate a person's level of intoxication. (*Chapter 3*)

Upselling or **upgrading** is offering a guest a call or premium brand of beer, wine, or spirits instead of a less expensive well or house brand. (*Chapter 3*)

Vasodilation occurs when alcohol causes the small blood vessels on the surface of the skin to dilate or swell, resulting in a loss of body heat. (*Chapter 1*)

Well or **house brands** are less expensive brands of beer, wine, and spirits. (*Chapter 3*)

Yellow, in the Traffic Light System, is when a guest becomes argumentative, talkative, or quieter, depending on the individual. Beverage alcohol service is slowed to one drink or less per hour. (*Chapter 3*)

ANSWER KEY

Chapter 1 Exercise

1. Which one of the following drinks has twice as much alcohol as the others?

   b) An 8-ounce glass of wine.

2. Most of the alcohol a person consumes is absorbed into the bloodstream from what part of the body?

   c) Small intestine.

3. Blood alcohol content or concentration (BAC) is the amount of:

   c) alcohol in the bloodstream.

4. Approximately how many drinks does the liver metabolize (break down) in one hour?

   a) One drink.

5. Alcohol does **not** affect the body by:

   b) stimulating the central nervous system.

6. Why does alcohol rapidly spread throughout the entire body once it has entered the bloodstream? Because alcohol:

   a) dissolves in water and can easily pass through cell walls.

7. What effect does fatty, high-protein food have on the body's absorption of alcohol into the bloodstream?

   a) It slows absorption by slowing the flow of alcohol into the small intestine.

8. A person would be at the highest risk for becoming intoxicated if he or she:

  b) is a small, depressed, dieting person with a high degree of body fat.

9. Which one of the following statements is **true**?

  b) Alcohol and drugs can be harmful when taken together.

10. What is the **most** important behavior to note when estimating a guest's alcohol consumption?

  c) Changing behaviors.

Chapter 2 Exercise

1. Which one of the following is the national trend in laws concerning drunk driving?

  b) Increasing the penalties for drunk driving.

2. Which one of the following statements is **false**? In some areas:

  b) minors can be served past the point of intoxication if they will not be driving when they leave the premises.

3. When an individual arrives at your establishment already intoxicated, what should you do?

  c) Do not serve the individual any beverage alcohol and keep him or her from driving away.

4. Establishments and their employees are **not** responsible for:

  b) charging too much for beverage alcohol.

5. What should you do if you become aware of illegal drug activity at your establishment?

  d) Immediately contact your manager.

6. Under what type of liability can your establishment be sued by a person injured by a drunk driver who became intoxicated at your establishment?

   a) Third-party liability.

7. In some states, the laws governing third-party liability in beverage alcohol-related cases are known as:

   c) dram shop laws.

8. Which one of the following statements is **false**?

   d) An establishment is **never** liable if it makes an honest mistake when serving beverage alcohol.

9. A court can hold a server liable for his or her:

   c) actual and constructive knowledge.

10. Which one of the following statements is **true**?

   a) Employees can be held liable if they fail to exercise reasonable care.

Chapter 3 Exercise

1. Which one of the following is **not** a valid form of ID?

   d) Birth certificate.

2. When checking IDs, the best procedure is to check:

   c) all guests IDs each time they enter.

3. What should doorstaff do when checking IDs?

   a) Be reasonable, friendly, and consistent.

4. When you have to refuse entrance to a minor, what should you say?

   b) "I'm sorry, but I can't let you in without a valid ID."

5. If you are serving beverage alcohol at a banquet or party, you should:

    b) carefully observe guests' behavioral changes.

6. To consistently serve beverage alcohol, you should:

    a) standardize drink recipes.

7. Upselling or upgrading means:

    d) offering a guest a call or premium brand of beverage alcohol.

8. When a guest has almost finished his or her present drink, what should you do?

    c) Wait until he or she has finished the present drink before offering another.

9. Your objective when serving guests in the yellow level is to:

    a) prevent them from reaching the red level.

10. How should you handle a guest in the red level?

    c) Stop beverage alcohol service.

Chapter 4 Exercise

1. If you have to discontinue beverage alcohol service to a guest, which one of the following should you do?

    a) Alert a backup about your decision, but speak to the guest by yourself.

2. What should you say to a guest when you are discontinuing beverage alcohol service?

    c) "I'm sorry, but our policies don't allow me to serve you any more beverage alcohol."

3. If an intoxicated guest becomes verbally abusive:

   d) get a manager.

4. If fighting or violence seems likely or occurs, you should immediately:

   b) alert a manager and call the police.

5. Which one of the following is **not** provided by establishments to ensure guests' automobile safety?

   b) One free alcohol beverage for designated drivers.

6. To prevent an intoxicated guest from driving away from your establishment, it is important for you to:

   a) get the guest's car keys.

7. If an intoxicated guest drives away from your establishment, what should you do?

   b) Immediately call the police and describe the guest and his or her car.

8. Which one of the following statements about designated driver programs is **false**?

   c) It is acceptable for other members of a group to become intoxicated if the designated driver stays sober.

9. When should you write an incident report?

   c) Immediately, so all details are clearly recorded.

10. Which one of the following situations does **not** require filling out an incident report?

    d) A minor is seated with adults who are drinking beverage alcohol.

NOTES

NOTES

NOTES